Written
and
Illustrated by:
T.F. Thompson
and
Ommi Lovice

ISBN-13: 978-0-692-16998-8
ISBN-10: 0-692-16998-9

Christmas Tree, Not for me!

Christmas Tree, not for me!
It's as pagan as can be!
"God created the evergreens," you might say, but he didn't intend for us to use them this way.

So when did decorating fir trees become cool?
It started with the Nordic celebration of Yule.

Germanic tribes like the Vikings who were
very strong and bold,
Praised the evergreen's resistance to the
winter cold.
The mistletoe, wreaths, and Yule log have
nothing to do with Christ,
These things were used in Nordic rituals for
prayer and sacrifice.

Statues, runes, treats, and clothes,
decorated the Norsemen's trees,
They hoped to entice the forest spirits
by leaving them as offerings.

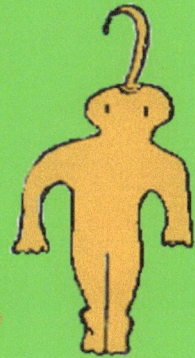

If you don't believe me, why don't you have a look,
Let's read what God says in his Good Book...

Thus saith the Lord, Learn not the way of the heathen, and be not dismayed at the signs of heaven; for the heathen are dismayed at them.

For the customs of the people are vain: for one cutteth a tree out of the forest, the work of the hands of the workman, with the axe.

They deck it with silver and with gold; they fasten it with nails and with hammers, that it move not.
Jeremiah 10: 2-4

So now you know about the Christmas tree and why it's pagan as can be, But don't stop here, this is just a pause The next book will be about Santa Clause...

Hey You!

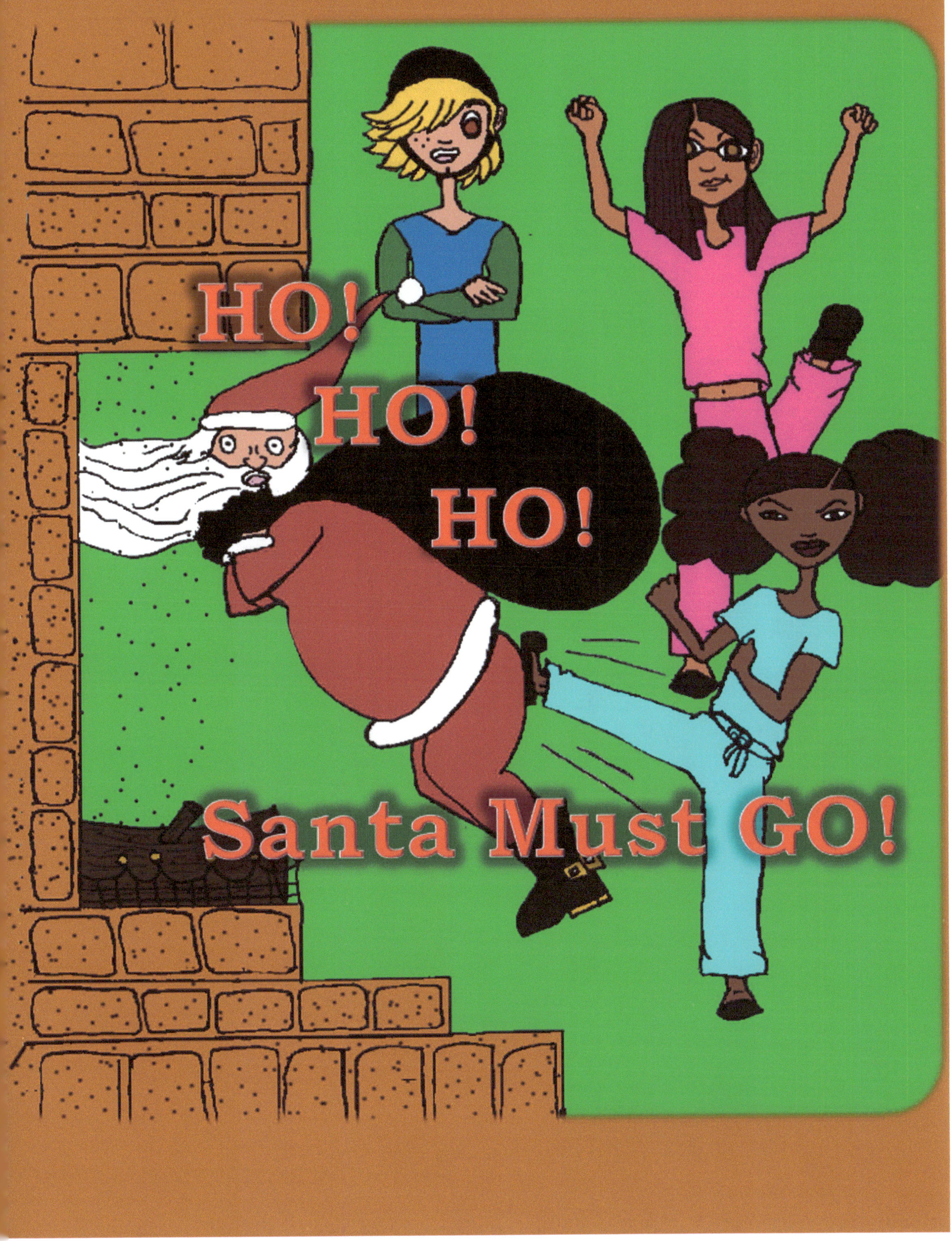
HO!
HO!
HO!
Santa Must GO!

Santa is not real I'm very sad to say,
Neither are his flying reindeer or his
big, red, wooden, sleigh.

Your parents work hard all year long to get your special gifts...

Sante laughs if you dreamt of him as you slept...

...Santa laughs as he sees your parents go into credit card debt...

Santa laughs and laughs as he is
given praise for nothing,
Believe me children, I'm not bluffing.

He sees you when you're sleeping...

He knows when you're awake...

He knows when you've been bad or good, so watch out for goodness sake!

So who is this imposter we give credit to on Christmas day?

He is a false spirit trying to steal
God's praise away.

So now you know the truth about Santa Clause
and all the confusion he has caused,

But still, there's one more book to go, the truth
about Christmas you must know...

The Truth About Christmas

You can look both high and low,
But not a word about Christ's birth
date in the Bible will show.

To understand how "Christmas" came to be, let's go back in time to about 336 AD..

The man that ordained the December 25th date, was the first Christian Emperor, Constantine the Great.

Constantine and other Pagans from north, south, east and west, were used to worshipping certain gods during the winter solstice.
The former pagan council chose for Christian to remember, a date nearest to the celebrations of their old gods, the 25th of December.

Greek god:
Dionysus

Roman god:
Attis

Egyptian god:
Horus

Persian god:
Mithra(s)

So what is Christmas now that we have made it plain to see,
A holiday made to trick you into worshipping false deities.

Now, if you're still confused on what
this whole thing is about,
I'll tell you in a nutshell; throw those
Christmas trees out!

Don't sing songs for Santa in hopes
that he'll show up that night,
And if he does I pray you'll give him
one heck of a fight.

On Christmas day, give back what other's have taken from God's creation. Honor your parents, and pray for members of each and every nation.

**Trust in God and worship him in spirit and in truth,
And don't forget to search for clues to find your own proof.**

We've done our best to show you the history behind the myths,
And that in all its glory is a very special gift

Be sure to worship our creator of heaven and of earth,
And the truth will be revealed to you if only you keep God first.

www.ingramcontent.com/pod-product-compliance
Lightning Source LLC
Chambersburg PA
CBHW042018090426
42811CB00015B/1680